KU-270-638

IT'S TRUE!

There Are Bugs
in Your Bed

Other  titles

Pigs Do Fly
Terry Denton PICTURES BY Terry Denton

Fashion Can Be Fatal
Susan Green PICTURES BY Gregory Rogers

Your Hair Grows 15 Kilometres a Year
Diana Lawrenson PICTURES BY Leigh Hobbs

Dinosaurs Never Died
John Long PICTURES BY Travis Tischler

Crime Doesn't Pay
Beverley MacDonald CARTOONS BY Andrew Weldon

A Bushfire Burned My Dunny Down
Tracey McGuire PICTURES BY Bill Wood

We Came From Slime
Ken McNamara PICTURES BY Andrew Plant

Frogs Are Cannibals
Michael Tyler PICTURES BY Mic Looby

The Romans Were the Real Gangsters
John & Joshua Wright PICTURES BY Joshua Wright

Heather Catchpole
and Vanessa Woods
PICTURES BY Craig Smith

IT'S TRUE!

There Are Bugs
in Your Bed

ALLEN&UNWIN

First published in 2004

Allen & Unwin
83 Alexander Street
Crows Nest NSW 2065
Australia
Phone: (61 2) 8425 0100
Fax: (61 2) 9906 2218
Email: info@allenandunwin.com
Web: www.allenandunwin.com

National Library of Australia
Cataloguing-in-Publication entry:

Catchpole, Heather.
It's true! There are bugs in your bed.
Bibliography.
Includes index.
ISBN 1 74114 299 7.
1. Insects – Juvenile literature. I. Woods, Vanessa.
II. Smith, Craig. III. Title.
595.7

Series, cover and text design by Ruth Grüner
Cover photograph: Gail Shumway/Getty Images
Set in 12.5pt Minion by Ruth Grüner
Printed by McPherson's Printing Group

3 5 7 9 10 8 6 4 2

**Teaching notes for the It's True! series are available
on the website: www.itstrue.com.au**

CONTENTS

WHY BUGS?

Did you realise that you are surrounded by bugs? Your back yard probably contains millions of creepy, crawly ants, beetles and centipedes, not to mention slippery earthworms, slugs and snails. And that's not all – your house is full of spiders, bedbugs and dust mites. These are weird and fascinating creatures. The Featherwing Beetle is so small you can hardly see it, but the Bird-eating Tarantula is as big as a dinner plate (imagine meeting that in the jungle!). Some bugs drink blood, others eat dead skin or cow poo. Some are complete pests (or dangerous), others are essential to our life on this planet. The bug world is full of surprises. Enter at your peril!

Heather Catchpole *Jan R Wood*

Chapter 1

Monsters in your bed

NIGHT-TIME BITERS

It's night and everyone in the house is asleep. Everyone?
Not quite. A blood-sucking monster with six legs,
a ghostly, transparent body and a huge appetite lives
in your bed. Sleep tight, but don't let the bedbugs bite!

Bedbugs like to snuggle up close to each other.
Hundreds of bedbugs can be found huddled together
for protection. They are small, about the size of an
extra large freckle, but that doesn't make them
any less monstrous.

Bedbugs hide in crevices, and come out to feed
on blood. Like all insects, they have six legs and three

main body parts, a head, a thorax (middle part), and an abdomen (back part). Being blood-suckers, they have strong mouth parts which look like a beak and can easily pierce your skin.

When a bedbug bites you, it injects saliva into the tiny wound on your skin. Its spit thins your blood, and numbs the area around the bite, so you don't notice. The spit also produces an itchy red welt that shows up soon after.

Bedbugs suck on their victims for two to three minutes. After they feed, they change colour. Their almost see-through skin turns brown-red as they fill up with blood, and their bodies become long and swollen. Although they'll feed daily given the chance, they may not feed again for a few weeks. In fact, they can go for a year without feeding at all.

Bedbugs feed on the blood of many warm-blooded animals, including humans, rats, guinea pigs, rabbits, bats and birds. They usually strike just before dawn, when their victim is asleep.

DUST-DWELLERS

Take a close look at the carpet by your bed. It's covered in a fine layer of dust. Kneel down and look closer still with a magnifying glass. Can you see it? It's got eight legs, a stomach and a mouth. It's a dust mite.

Dust mites are less than a quarter of a millimetre long, almost impossible for us to see. But they do have a big effect; dust mites are one of the main causes of allergies in humans. There are probably thousands of dust mites in your house.

Dust mites eat dead skin. You, your family and your pets shed skin all the time without noticing (have a look under your bed and you'll see some).

Tiny bits brush off your body and collect in the dust around the house, particularly in the bedroom. Household dust can also contain fungi, mould, pollen grains and bacteria, as well as insect bodies (like carpet beetles, silverfish, clothes moths and cockroaches).

Dust mites are not insects, they are more closely related to spiders and ticks. Under a microscope, a dust mite looks truly terrifying, with eight spindly legs, a huge stomach and a tiny head. In fact, these tiny creatures are mostly harmless, although in some people dust mites can cause hay fever, skin irritations and even asthma attacks.

The reason for all the sneezing, wheezing, itching and scratching isn't the dust mites themselves, but what they add to dust. As dust mites grow, they poo, and they shed *their* skin. It's the dust-mite poo and the flakes of skin shed by dust mites that causes allergic reactions in people.

Dust mites are mostly found in the bedroom, but they can snuggle into and live in the carpet, the couch or a mattress. We carry them around from room to room or even from house to house on our clothes.

Dust mites live anywhere there are people, which is
pretty much all over the world.

BLOOD-SUCKING VAMPIRES

Yeeeee-ow.
As you close
your eyes ready
to sink into sleep,
a blood-sucking
vampire circles above
your head. She makes
a high buzzing sound caused
by beating her wings 300–800 times
a second, as she aims her needle-like
mouth and prepares to attack.

Only female mosquitoes suck blood.
Blood from humans, other mammals and reptiles
helps mosquitoes' eggs develop. The females bite only
when it is time to lay their eggs. The rest of the time,
females and males drink nectar from flowers,
just like bees.

The female uses her sharp mouth parts to pierce the skin of her prey. As she does this, she squirts a bit of her spit in to keep the blood flowing. Like the bedbug, she has a chemical in her spit that makes us itch.

Mosquitoes don't have wings all their lives. When they hatch, they live in water. The females lay eggs in calm ponds, lakes, rivers, or even in puddles. The hatching mosquito larvae are called 'wrigglers' because they wriggle a lot. They have a siphon, like a snorkel, which they use to breathe air. When they get bigger, they stop eating and develop a hard outer case called a pupa, just as caterpillars form a chrysalis to become butterflies. When the mosquito breaks out of the pupa, it sits on the case until its body and wings have hardened and dried, then it flies away.

Have you noticed that some people always get bitten by mosquitoes, while other people never do? Female mosquitoes are attracted by a combination of warmth, colour and smell. Everyone has a different smell, and mosquitoes are attracted to some people's smell more than others.

Although females may only bite a few times in their

lifetime, mosquitoes are the most dangerous creatures on Earth. This is because some species can carry deadly diseases such as malaria. Malaria is a parasite. Parasites feed on other creatures, which are called hosts, and the host usually ends up becoming sick or dying. The malaria parasite is a microscopic creature that lives inside the stomach of the female mosquito and then moves into the part of her mouth where spit is formed. When the mosquito bites, the parasites in her spit travel into the bloodstream of the animal she has bitten. The malaria parasite then makes its way to the liver, multiplies and makes an infected person very sick. If another mosquito bites the infected person, it may swallow some malaria parasites and go on to infect another person.

In Australia, mosquitoes are more of a pest than a deadly threat. Malaria exists in tropical countries such as Africa, South America and South-east Asia, and kills over a million people each year. It currently doesn't exist in Australia. Normally, we can stay pretty safe by covering up at dusk, using mosquito repellents, and slapping hard when we feel that little jab!

FLEAS: SUPER ATHLETES

With a jump, a hop and a skip, the flea has bounced into the insect book of records as one of the world's best high-jumpers. Using their hairy, muscular back legs, fleas can hop an incredible 18 centimetres high and 33 centimetres long. If they were the size of a human, that would be a jump of 76 metres high and 130 metres long – 15 times as high and as far as the world's best athletes can jump.

These super-insects have another special power – they are almost unsquashable. Pinch a flea between your fingers and it will hop away unharmed. Fleas are difficult to crush because of their hard bodies.

Even a bath won't get rid of fleas – ask any dog. In fact, the only way to make your pet flea-free is by using a special flea collar, powder, shampoo or solution.

There's a good reason for not wanting to have Fido carry the local flea circus. Not only do fleas feed on pets and their owners, leaving tiny itchy welts, but fleas can also carry parasites and diseases. The famous bubonic plague of the 1300s was probably spread across Europe by fleas that lived on rats. Other rat fleas carried typhus fever into Asia. If accidentally eaten (yuk!), fleas can pass on the parasitic tapeworm. (There's more about tapeworms in Chapter 8.)

Fleas have three pairs of legs. They can jump so high because their hind or back legs are enlarged, helping them to make a quick getaway. They have narrow bodies that enable them to move easily between hair, fur or feathers. Their super-sharp mouth can pierce the thick skin of animals thousands of times their size. If this isn't enough to put them in the ugly book of records, some fleas also have spiky spines and bristles on their cheeks.

A flea starts off as an egg. In one month a single female flea can produce almost 1000 eggs. In any flea infestation, half of the fleas are still at the egg stage, so if you think your pet has a lot of fleas, just imagine how many more are waiting to hatch.

Fleas develop first as larvae – squiggly, white, worm-like creatures which feed off bits of shed skin, as well as tiny insects and other creatures. Some flea larvae even eat the digested blood found in an adult flea's poo. After a while, flea larvae spin themselves a silken cocoon, which soon becomes covered in the hair, dust and dirt in which they live. They live in the cocoon until they re-form into adult fleas. The vibration from a footstep, the heat of a body pressing on them, or the smell of someone's breath tells them that dinner is nearby. They spend most of their time on the furniture and only hop onto your dog for a quick snack – meals on legs.

Fleas can survive without eating for up to a year, so you can imagine the horde of hungry high-jumpers waiting for you to come back from your next holiday.

Chapter 2

Gunk in your bathroom

SLIME

It's gooey, dripping, smelly, sticky, yucky and
sometimes green. No, it's not snot – it's slime!

So just what is slime? Slime is an oozy stuff made by
tiny life forms too small for us to see. Mould, fungi and
algae are the slime that live in bathrooms.

Green and brown slime is usually algae. Algae were
among the first things alive on Earth. As far as we
know, they don't do much except hang around being
slimy. They are plants made of only one or a few cells.
(Cells are tiny and make up anything that is alive.
We have billions of cells in our bodies.)

You might find green algae in a swimming pool if it's not cleaned regularly. They have a slimy feel and a bright green colour and they either float freely or hang onto the sides.

Yellow or brown algae are often found in aquariums. They form a thin layer of yellowy-brown slimy stuff on the surfaces of an aquarium if it's not kept clean.

Have you ever noticed little black spots on the tiles in your bathroom? They may seem innocent enough, but did you know they are alive? Black algae form the black spots between bathroom tiles, and in

Millions of algae cells make up each black spot

the silicon that seals off the bottom of the shower or bath. Millions of individual algae cells make up each black spot. The top layer of the algae spot is tough and protects the layers underneath from all the bathroom cleaners you can pour on it.

Living in the dampness in your bathroom walls are strange growths called mould. Mould is a fuzzy growth made up of tiny, tiny life forms called fungi.

(They're distantly related to mushrooms.) The fungi are so small they live on particles found in the air, and they invade bathroom walls and ceilings wherever water gets into the plaster. These fungi existed on our planet billions of years before we did, and they now live all around us. They grow on our food, making bread go furry. Other moulds make slimy black stains on your bathroom ceiling. They could be above your bathtub right now.

Next time you go to the bathroom look around to see how much microscopic life you're sharing it with!

MAKE SLIME

Here's how to make a cool, slimy substance that has some surprises.

You'll need: • some cornflour • some water • green food colouring • a mixing bowl

1 Pour the cornflour into the mixing bowl.

2 Stir in water a little bit at a time until the cornflour has become a very thick paste.

3 Stir in five drops of green food colouring.

4 Dribble a little bit of your home-made slime off the spoon. It should be runny.

5 Grab a handful of slime, and throw it into the sink or onto a surface that can be cleaned. When it hits the surface, the slime is like a solid ball! It's solid because of the way the tiny particles of cornflour respond to the pressure of the impact. Try punching the slime – it feels solid. Now move your hand slowly through it – the slime feels like a liquid again!

SLUGS IN YOUR SHOWER

It's true; slugs can crawl up shower drains. Next time you have a shower, see if one has crawled up your drain, and is sliding slimily towards you. It could be as long as your finger, have an orange, red, brown or black body, and leave a trail of slime behind it. If you step on it, it will go *squish*!

Snails and slugs are mostly plant-eaters, but some are carnivorous (meat-eaters). We usually find them in the garden, where their favourite foods include lettuce and cabbage leaves. They prefer cloudy, rainy days and love moving around at night. Walk down the garden path after a downpour – it's hard not to crunch snails underfoot. Gross!

On sunny days, snails seal off their shell to prevent themselves from drying out. Slugs slink off in search of somewhere slimy, and that's why you might find one sliding up your shower drain.

Snails and slugs have one enormous foot along the length of their body, and it secretes slimy mucus that helps them glide along the ground.

The mucus dries and leaves a silvery slime trail behind them. On a wet day you can see a network of slime trails as the snails and slugs criss-cross the path.

Boy or girl? Snails and slugs are hermaphrodites (herm-aphro-dytes), meaning they are male and female at the same time. They live for three to six months, and lay batches of eggs on the underside of leaves and in soil cracks in the garden. These look like tiny crystal globes. There are probably hundreds in your garden right now.

The Giant Garden Slug is the longest slug in the world at 20 centimetres long. It lives for up to three years, and hunts other slugs!

ToILET TERRORS

Have you ever wondered why you have to wash your hands after you go to the toilet, even if they look clean?

Covering nearly every surface on Earth are billions of creatures so small we can't even see them. They are called bacteria.

Bacteria have been around for more than 3500 million years, longer than any other living creature. There are bacteria everywhere, from volcanoes deep in the ocean to the clouds above our heads, and even in our mouths and tummies.

Bacteria eat almost everything, but they don't have mouths as we do. Instead, they make special chemicals to chop up food into tiny little pieces which the bacteria then grab and suck through their skin.

There are so many different species of bacteria that it's impossible to count them all. There might be several million in your back yard alone. Most bacteria won't hurt you, and without bacteria we would not be able to survive. All plants and animals depend on bacteria. There are bacteria in our stomachs that help us digest our food. Plants have bacteria on their roots which help them get food from the soil. Bacteria can even fight diseases caused by other bacteria.

Some bacteria live in poo. In an amount of poo weighing less than a sheet of paper, there are as many as 100 000 000 000 bacteria (that's 100 billion). Some of these bacteria are harmless while they are living in our bodies, but make us sick if we poo them out then accidentally eat them again. (Eeew!) You can imagine that if you don't wash your hands after you go to the toilet, some bacteria could end up on your hands, then in your food the next time you make a sandwich.

For some animals the bacteria in poo are very important. Ringtail possums eat eucalyptus leaves which are very tough and hard to digest. The possums have bacteria in their stomachs which help digest the eucalyptus leaves, but even the bacteria can't break it all down the first time. The eucalyptus leaves pass through the digestive system and come out as poo, and the possum eats its poo so the bacteria can have another go at digesting the leaves. When baby ringtail possums become old enough to eat eucalyptus leaves, they eat some of their mother's poo (which has the bacteria in it) so then they can have the same bacteria in their stomachs.

Humans don't have this kind of bacteria, so don't try this at home. The only thing that will happen if you eat your poo is that you will get sick. So after the toilet, wash your hands – with soap!!

Chapter 3

Kitchen Creatures

THE HEADLESS HUNTER

They eat the labels off containers and the bindings off books. They love toilets and sewers. They move at night and hide during the day, and some of them live in trees or caves. They can even live for up to a month without their heads. They are cockroaches.

Don't even bother swatting these kitchen monsters – their strong armoured skin and flattened bodies protect them. They'll just scuttle away to come back again another day. In fact, they are almost indestructible – some people say that they could survive nuclear war.

Cockroaches are omnivores, which means they eat plants and animal food. In fact, they eat anything they can chew on and being scavengers, they usually eat bits and pieces they find lying around.

If you are extremely lucky, you might see a rare white cockroach. If you can catch it, put it in a container, then come back a few hours later. Mysteriously, in the place of the white cockroach, there will be an ordinary brown cockroach. What happened? You caught the cockroach just when it had shed its hard armoured skin, called an exoskeleton. The exoskeleton doesn't stretch, so when the cockroach grows bigger, it has to shed its old skin and grow a new one. Before the new skin hardens, the cockroach appears white.

What about a headless cockroach? Cockroaches can survive for a while without their head because they breathe through a system of tubes attached to small openings on their body. These openings deliver oxygen straight to their cells. We breathe through our mouth and nose, and the oxygen is delivered to our cells by our blood. Cockroaches also have very low blood pressure, so if they lose their heads, blood doesn't spurt out uncontrollably. Also, like most insects, cockroaches can go for a long time without eating.

Believe it or not, native Australian cockroaches are very attractive insects. They have an amazing variety of patterns to keep them camouflaged in the bush. They can flatten their bodies to slip into the smallest spaces, or simply stay still and blend into their environment. The heaviest cockroach in the world is Queensland's Giant Burrowing Cockroach, which grows as big as your fist.

The two biggest pests are the German Cockroach, which is small and brown, and the American Cockroach, which is big and black – it can be more than 5 cm long! The pale brown ones running around your kitchen are probably German cockroaches. Two reasons not to love the German Cockroach are that it both spits and goes to the toilet on the food in your cupboard.

The large black cockroaches usually found outside Australian homes are invaders from America. These are the largest of the common cockroaches and are found all over the world. On summer nights you can hardly go a step without trampling on one. But if you only step on its head, the cockroach will be fine!

ITTY BITTY WARRIORS

You're crunching your favourite breakfast cereal and you suddenly see a line of tiny black bodies marching towards the bowl. Small and unstoppable, ants are **everywhere**!

The tiny black ants you find in your kitchen live in nests which contain a queen, eggs, larvae and hundreds of worker ants. All of the worker ants are female, and each worker ant has a different job, such as looking after the eggs, feeding the larvae, collecting food, or defending the nest from intruders. In some ant species there are soldier ants with enormous heads and huge jaws that crush alien ants invading the nest.

The common black ants found outdoors are called meat ants. They build large, gravel-covered nests which usually house around 2000 ants, though nests have been found with more than half a million. In an area of the Australian bush as big as your school oval, you could find 20 million ants! The longest ant in the world is the Australian Bulldog Ant. It grows about as big as your little finger!

ANT TRAILS

Next time you find a line of ants, try this:
carefully place a thin strip of cardboard across
the line, and watch what happens. Ants use
pheromones to leave a trail for the next ant to
follow. The cardboard breaks the line, and it takes
the ants a while to pick up the signal again.
After a few ants have crossed the cardboard,
the trail is re-formed.

Try taking
the cardboard
away again.
Ant
confusion!

Ants are attracted to meat, sweets, fats and oils. They will search indoors for water during dry periods. Once they find something they want, ants leave a trail of chemicals called pheromones (feer-o-mones). The pheromones tell their nest-mates that there's something good to be found. Soon, hundreds of ants are marching forth, forming trails from food scraps to the cracks in the walls and floors.

Adult ants eat only liquid food. They suck liquid from their prey or drink waste liquids produced by other insects such as aphids and scale insects. This food is then vomited to feed other adult ants. Though this sounds a bit gross, it means those ants who are working inside the nest can concentrate on their jobs, and they don't have to find food as well. Solid food, such as your cereal crumbs, is carried back to the nest to feed the larvae.

SHOO FLY, DON'T BOTHER ME

Buzzzzzz off! Even the sound of one is enough to drive you into a swatting frenzy. Bzzz. **Bzzz!**

Flies are one of Australia's most annoying house guests. Every summer, hundreds of house flies land on your food, and walk around on your ceiling.

A house fly beats its wings over 20 000 times a minute. It uses hairy, micro-hooking, glue-oozing toe pads to walk upside-down on the ceiling.

These spongy toe pads are the fly's taste buds. Flies walk over their food to check out its flavour, and they smell using their antennae. And did you know that flies take off *backwards*?

Flies have the grossest table manners. They can only eat liquids. So what do they do when they find solid food? They spit on it! Their spit turns solid stuff into a mushy soup, and then they slurp it up. Yuk!

At least house flies aren't too big. Australia's longest fly, the Robber Fly, can grow up to 8 centimetres long.

Like most other insects, flies begin as eggs, and grow into larvae. They then make themselves a pupal shell in which they develop into adult flies. Fly larvae are creamy-white, worm-like maggots.

FLY-BLOWN OR FLY-BITTEN?

As with mosquitoes, it's only the female flies that bite. Biting flies such as the March Fly and Horse Fly might take a quick snack from you to get the extra energy they need to lay eggs.

Some maggots bite too! March Fly maggots even inject venom into their prey to paralyse it so they can suck its insides out.

Blowfly maggots are a big problem for farmers. Sheep can become 'fly-blown', which means maggots are eating away the sheep's flesh. Maggots have their uses, though. In the olden days, an injured person's wounds could become infected, or even green and rotten. Maggots put on the wound cleaned away infected flesh. Often no further treatment was needed.

Bush Fly maggots prefer moist, warm cow poo to grow up in. In areas of Australia where there's a lot of cow poo, and therefore lots of maggots, people introduced dung beetles to try and reduce the number of flies. Dung beetles bury poo as food for their own baby dung beetles. By burying the maggots' favourite food, the little dung beetle has helped the Bush Fly to buzz off!

Chapter 4

Garden grommits

Beetles, beetles, beetles! There are more types of beetles than any other animals in the world. In fact, one animal in every four is a beetle. They are everywhere, even underwater in lakes and rivers.

Scientists believe they are so successful at surviving because they are so well protected.

Beetles' front wings have over time developed a hard casing called the elytra, which closes in a straight line down the beetles' backs. This protects their soft wings. It helps keep the beetles safe from predators (creatures that eat them from the outside in) and parasites (creatures that eat them from the inside out). The elytra also reduces the amount of water beetles lose, and can keep them cool in extreme conditions, such as in the desert. Some beetles are flattened, which means they can crawl into the smallest, safest places.

Beetles have been around for about 350 million years, and in that time, they've developed into some of the strongest and strangest creatures around.

BEETLE BOOK OF RECORDS

Strongest   The African Scarab Beetle, also called the Rhinoceros Beetle, is the strongest animal in the world. It can lift objects 850 times its own weight!

Biggest   The biggest Australian beetle is the Wallace Longhorn Beetle. Its body is as big as your hand and its antennae are further apart than the length of your school ruler! It's found on the Cape York Peninsula, where its larvae burrow into fig trees.

Longhorn beetles have antennae up to three times their body length. Like extra-long arms, the antennae let the beetle sense things around a wider area.

Longest   The world record for length is held by the Brazilian Longhorn Beetle, an amazing 20 centimetres long.

Heaviest   A Goliath Beetle weighs up to 100 grams, which is about as heavy as a large apple.

Smallest   The Featherwing Beetle is the smallest beetle. It's only a quarter of a millimetre long.

THE ODD BODS of BEETLEDOM

Gross eaters

Dung beetles live entirely on poo. They lay their eggs in poo, dig their burrows under poo, and of course they eat poo too. For humans, and many other animals, dung beetles are quite helpful. The large numbers of cattle introduced to Australia during the last 200 years have produced lots of cow poo. Native dung beetles, which are used to the small pellets of dung produced by native animals, were unable to deal with the enormous cow poos, so African Dung Beetles were introduced. African

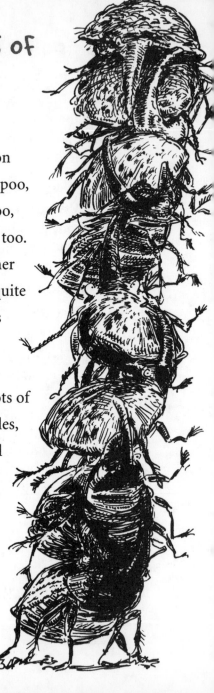

Dung Beetles break up cow poo, roll it into small balls and bury it to feed their babies. This has resulted in more poo-free pastures, which has helped to reduce the number of flies.

Bottom-blasting beetles

Have you ever eaten a whole lot of beans and later felt some explosive after-effects – or lived with someone who did? If you've been at the wrong end of a gas attack, then you know just how it feels to be the victim of a Bombardier Beetle!

Bombardier Beetles defend themselves with a blast of a boiling hot, toxic chemical spray. The spray is secreted in a special gland in the Bombardier Beetle's bottom. When a predator attacks, the Bombardier Beetle bends over and lets rip. The chemicals in the spray react to form an explosive mixture which is released with an audible *pop* sound. Talk about bad gas!

Lovely Ladybird Beetles

Lots of tiny black spots on a shiny red, orange or yellow back – it's a lovely Ladybird Beetle. Up close it appears to be dead – it's lying on its back, and there's yellow stuff leaking from its legs. The yellow stuff is to fool predators. Things are not what they seem. The Ladybird Beetle is only playing dead, and it's not so lovely after all.

To an aphid, mealybug or scale insect, a Ladybird Beetle is a vicious predator. In fact, Ladybird Beetle larvae eat so many aphids (50 to 200 per day) that they are often used as a natural pesticide to keep rose bushes and other plants free from the pesky green aphids. They might look pretty to us, but Ladybird Beetles are an aphid's worst nightmare.

THE SECRET LIFE OF A CHRISTMAS BEETLE

Every year, from late spring to mid-summer, hundreds of thousands of Christmas Beetles appear. Where do they all come from?

As baby beetles, or grubs, Christmas Beetles spend autumn and winter under the ground, feeding on rotting plant material. During this time they mature into adults. They remain buried in the ground until falling rain makes the soil soft enough for the Christmas Beetles to dig themselves out. That's why you'll see lots of Christmas Beetles just after a summer storm. They can appear in their thousands, stripping their favourite gum trees of leaves.

COLLECTING BEETLES

You'll need: • a large empty tin
• three bamboo skewers • some stickytape
• a piece of cardboard a bit bigger than
the end of the tin • a magnifying glass

1 Find a clean, empty tin.
(Watch out for the sharp sides.)

2 Ask an adult to help you poke some
drainage holes in the bottom of the tin.

3 Dig a small hole in the ground and put the
tin in it. Make sure the edges of the tin don't
stick up above ground. This is a pit trap to catch
unsuspecting beetles.

4 Make a roof for your pit trap by cutting
a circle of white card, slightly larger than the tin.
Stick three skewers through the card so that they
are evenly spaced around the edge of the circle,
and hold them in place using stickytape.
Place this over the pit trap like a roof to keep
out the rain.

5 Check your pit trap several times a day,
and release any bugs you've caught after you've
observed them through the magnifying glass.
All insects are important
to the environment.

PESTS oR GUESTS

The Confused Flour Beetle is one of many types of beetle that are unwelcome guests inside huge vats of stored grain. (Talking of confusion, the creature we call a 'firefly' is actually a beetle. These beetles' abdomens glow in the dark, when chemicals made by them combine with air.)

Another pest, the Cigarette Beetle, has a serious tobacco-chewing problem. It also leaves small circular holes in plastic, paper and cardboard packaging.

Beetles were eating their way through Queensland's sugar-cane crop in the 1920s, and that's why cane toads were introduced to Australia. The toads were no use at controlling the beetles, and now the cane toads are a much bigger pest.

Chapter 5

Blue-blooded monsters

Imagine you are a fly, happily buzzing through the air, in search of some garbage to lay your eggs in. Suddenly, you become stuck in mid-air. You frantically flap your wings but you are held on all sides by invisible threads as strong as steel. The threads begin to tremble as a furry monster walks towards you.

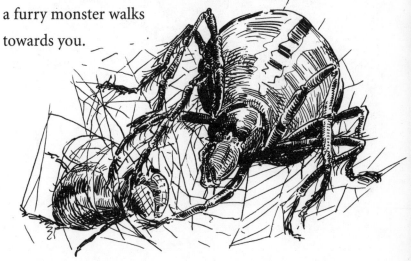

As the monster comes closer, you see her fangs are curved like two sabre-tooth-tiger teeth. You think she's going to chomp you up right away, but instead she taps you all over with her long furry legs and shoots something at you from her bottom. It's strong and sticky, and it wraps around you so tightly that you can't move.

Being eaten by a spider must be a terrifying experience. Luckily, spiders don't eat humans, and they will only bite us if they are defending themselves.

A spider pierces its prey with its fangs and injects venom. This venom interrupts messages that the brain sends to the muscles; the muscles can't move and the prey is paralysed. The spider then vomits up digestive juices which dissolve the prey and turn its insides into soup, which the spider slurps up. If you look carefully at a spider web you may see the shell-like exoskeleton of an insect that was the spider's last meal.

Spiders don't have ears or noses. Instead, they have fine hairs on their bodies that they use to hear, smell and taste. Sound is made up of tiny vibrations that move through the air. The hair on a spider's body senses these vibrations and allows the spider to 'hear' what is happening. On the end of a spider's legs are special hairs that can smell and taste. So when a spider turns its prey over with its legs, what it's really doing is tasting its victim!

Spider blood is blue. This is because the blood has copper in it which gives a bluish colour. Ours has iron in it, which makes it red. Spiders don't have veins like us. Instead, blood fills up the body like a bath for organs such as the heart and stomach.

The most fascinating thing about spiders is probably their webs. A spider spins silk with spinnerets, special body parts which are at the end of its abdomen, between the back legs. Spider silk may look fragile, but it is stronger than a piece of steel of the same thickness, and it is also very elastic.

Orb spiders, which spin spiral webs, have different kinds of silk. One is a non-sticky silk that the spider lays down first, pointing outwards from the centre in all directions. The spider walks on these non-sticky threads. Another kind of silk is sticky and runs in a spiral from the centre of the web outward. It is this sticky thread that will trap the prey. Finally, there is the silk that the spider uses to wrap the prey that's been caught in the web.

In some spider families, the females are much bigger than the males. If the male is on the female's web, she could mistake him for an insect and eat him. This is a problem because somehow, the male must mate with the female. He very cautiously approaches the female, usually making some sort of signal, like plucking the web, so she will know he is not an insect.

After mating, he will try to escape, but sometimes she eats him anyway. This gives her extra energy before she lays her eggs.

NETTING AND KNITTING

Now for some spider trivia.

- Net-casting spiders weave small webs, which they carry around between their legs and throw over passing prey.

- Polynesian fishermen use the thread of the Golden Orb-weaving Spider as fishing line.

- In 1709 a scientist called Bon de Saint-Hilaire made socks and gloves from spiderwebs. About 65 000 spider cocoons were needed for one sock. Hilarious!

REDBACK SPIDERS

Redback spiders are probably Australia's most famous spiders. The female is only one centimetre long, but her bite is venomous enough to kill a small child or animal. Luckily, there is anti-venom that is an antidote to the venom.

Redback spiders used to be very common in country toilets. One of the scariest things about going to the outside toilet at night was the possibility of being bitten on the bottom. These days redbacks live in dry, dark places such as under logs or bark, but can sometimes be found in people's garages and sheds or under floorboards. Redbacks usually eat insects but can also eat other spiders or even small lizards that get tangled in their webs.

DADDY LONGLEGS

You probably wouldn't even
feel a Daddy Longlegs bite
you. Daddy Longlegs are
quite harmless. They build
messy webs and if they
are disturbed, they vibrate
their web violently so that it
becomes invisible. Daddy Longlegs are one of the most
common house spiders, and are found in houses all
over the world.

Much more fearsome-looking, but just as harmless,
is the Huntsman Spider. It is very hairy and can grow
as big as an adult's hand. Huntsmen often visit our
houses and cars.

SYDNEY FUNNELWEB SPIDER

Australia has many venomous spiders, including the
Sydney Funnelweb. This is one of the most venomous
spiders in the world. The male's bite is more dangerous

than the female's, because the venom of the male contains a chemical that is particularly dangerous to humans. It can kill us. The venom affects only primates (apes and humans), and does not harm other mammals like cats and dogs. Funnelwebs live in moist, cool places such as under rocks, or in rotting logs. They leave a tripline of silk outside their burrows to alert them to mates, prey or intruders.

BIRD-EATER

The Goliath Bird-eating Tarantula is the biggest spider in the world. It's about the size of a dinner plate! It doesn't spin a web; instead the spider ambushes and bites its prey with its huge fangs. The spider is big enough to eat frogs, toads, lizards, mice and even

small snakes.

To defend themselves, tarantulas have tiny hairs on their backs with sharp tips. If they are being attacked, tarantulas will kick off a cloud of these hairs, which causes an irritating rash.

Tarantulas were named after a town called Taranto in Italy. Every summer for 300 years, a strange sickness broke out, and the townspeople thought the sickness was because of the bite of a large hairy Wolf Spider that became known as the Tarantula. The real culprit was a European relative of the Redback Spider.

Chapter 6

creatures that bite and sting

BEES – A FLOWER'S BEST FRIENDS

Did you know that honey is bee vomit?

To make honey, honey bees first vomit up the nectar they have collected from flowers. Then they swirl it around in their mouths to remove some of the water. The thick syrupy nectar that's left is called honey. One bee makes a teaspoon and a half of honey in its lifetime.

Bees that collect nectar are female, and they live in a hive with a queen who lays the eggs. Male bees cannot sting and they live only long enough to mate with the queen, and then they die.

When a worker bee has found a good source of nectar, she returns to the hive and performs a 'waggle' dance, which is secret bee language telling the other bees where the flowers are. The length of the dance and the number of 'waggles' describes how far away the flowers are, and the direction of the dance describes where the flowers are in relation to the sun. If the flowers are in the same direction as the sun, the bee dances straight up.

If the flowers are away from the sun, the bee dances straight down. If the flowers are to the left of the sun, the bee dances to the left, and so on.

Bravo!

To help them find flowers, bees have five eyes. Three eyes are on top of their head and are sensitive to light so that bees can tell exactly where the sun is, even on a cloudy day. The other two eyes are larger and can detect pictures, colour and movement.

Bees don't see the world the way we do. Bees detect small changes in movement better than humans because their brain and eyes process information much faster. Bees can't see red, but they can see colours that we can't see, such as ultraviolet. Ultraviolet light is what causes sunburn. The ultraviolet markings on flowers catch the bees' attention and show them where to find the nectar.

When the bee visits a flower, she brushes against the flower's pollen. Then she carries the pollen to another flower. This fertilises the flower and lets it make seeds. Without bees, many flowers couldn't make seeds. In fact, a third of all our plant food is pollinated by bees. We couldn't live without them.

Then again, some people could live without bee stings. These hurt because the bee stingers inject a chemical called melittin, which stimulates pain receptors in our skin. The pain lasts from a few minutes to several days. Some people have such a strong reaction to the chemical that they can die from it.

The best thing about bees is definitely the honey. Bee vomit on toast? Yum.

AIR-CONDITIONED LIVING

If it's getting too hot at the hive, bees have their own air-conditioning. A few workers stay at the entrance of the hive and fan droplets of water with their wings to cool the air.

If it gets too cold, thousands of workers gather around the queen in a big ball. The bees on the outside of the ball form a very tight layer to keep out the cold, and the bees on the inside eat honey to give them energy and then shiver their wing muscles to create heat.

WASPISH BEHAVIOUR

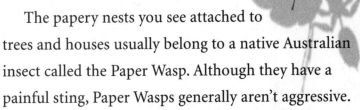

If you see a papery nest hanging
under the eaves of your house,
then it's a sure sign you've got
visitors. Watch out for wasps!

The papery nests you see attached to
trees and houses usually belong to a native Australian
insect called the Paper Wasp. Although they have a
painful sting, Paper Wasps generally aren't aggressive.

Have you ever chewed up some paper to make a
spitball? A Paper Wasp's nest is made of chewed-up
plant fibres stuck together with wasp spit. The wasps
build their nests in hidden places, such as hollows in
logs, underground, and under house eaves.

Like bees, Paper Wasps have a nest that houses
a queen and many workers. All the workers are female,
with the males only living for a short period of time.
After the males have mated with the queen, they die.
If there are several queens in the nest, one queen may
take some workers and fly off somewhere to build
a new nest.

Adult wasps feed on plant nectar, but attack and kill caterpillars, which they chop up into tiny pieces to feed to their larvae. This could be useful to you if you have lots of caterpillars in your garden that munch on your vegetables.

One unwelcome wasp that lives in Australia is the European Wasp. It probably entered Australia by stowing away in a ship. It's a serious pest, and is also very dangerous. If you see one, keep clear.

European Wasps look like bees, but they have brighter yellow markings and are slightly bigger. They also have black spots along their abdomen, or middle (the wasp's stomach).

Like the Paper Wasps, European Wasps make their nests in secret places – in the ground, in trees or in spaces behind walls and ceilings. They have a painful sting, which can be dangerous if it causes a serious allergic reaction, or if you are stung in the mouth or throat. European Wasps have a much easier time than native Australian wasps because they have no natural predators in Australia.

A STINGING ATTACK

Wasps are different from bees. A bee dies after it has used its sting, but a wasp can sting repeatedly.

In many species of wasps, the females are flightless but they can still sting and attack large prey – even Huntsman Spiders. The largest Australian wasp, with a wingspan of up to 7 centimetres, is called a Spider Wasp and – you guessed it – preys on spiders.

Native wasps won't attack unless their home is threatened.

WASP STINGS

If you are stung by a wasp, the area around the sting will become painful, red and swollen. In most cases, the swelling goes down after a few hours, but the area stays red and itchy for a few days. Some people have a more severe reaction to stings, and need to go to a doctor immediately.

FLOWER POWER!

One Australian wasp has an evil twin in the form of an
Australian orchid. This orchid mimics the appearance
of the wasp, and also mimics the chemical signals used
by wasps to communicate, called pheromones.

The flower looks and smells exactly like a female wasp.
When it's mating time, most of the male wasps land on
the flowers instead of finding a partner, which helps the
flower to spread its pollen. Sneaky!

MANY-LEGGED MONSTERS

Q: What goes clippety-clippety-CLOMP, clippety-clippety-CLOMP, clippety-clippety-CLOMP?

A: A centipede with a walking stick.

Actually, centipedes are more likely to go clippety-clippety-CHOMP, as they tear into their latest victims with their huge, venomous claws. Centipedes are deadly predators!

Centipedes don't have a hundred legs, as their name suggests (*centi*=hundred and *ped*=foot). They have many-segmented bodies, with one pair of legs for each body segment. Their front legs are more like jaws. These jaw-like legs are venomous, allowing centipedes to attack creatures as large as birds and mice, although they're more likely to make a meal of an insect. Luckily centipedes are too small to be a danger to humans.

The biggest centipedes are as long and as wide as a school ruler. The most legs a centipede has is 177 pairs. That's 354 legs! A common garden centipede has fewer than 20 pairs of legs.

Millipedes are actually very different from centipedes, and are quite harmless to us. Millipedes have two pairs of legs for each body segment, so they might have more legs than a centipede, but no millipede has 1000 legs, despite the name (*milli*=thousand). No millipede has more than 750 legs.

Millipedes have to be very careful not to trip over their own feet. The two legs on the same side of one body segment move in different directions – one moves back while the other moves forward. That's why millipedes are such slow walkers. Try crawling on your hands and knees, and move your right arm forward while your right leg moves backward. Move the left leg and left arm in the same way. Now imagine you had another 746 limbs that moved like that!

Millipedes don't bite, but they can exude a poisonous substance that kills tiny creatures that come in contact with them, and can cause allergic reactions in humans.

chapter 7

Squirmy, slimy things

WEIRD, WIGGLY WORMS

Squirmy and slimy, with no arms, legs, eyes, nose or lungs; worms are some of the weirdest things you'll find in the garden.

Worms breathe through their skin, and they have to be damp to survive. They produce a sticky, slimy substance as they move. Worms move by wriggling along on tiny hairs found on each of the 32 segments or muscular rings that make up their bodies (it's true – worms aren't bald!). These muscular rings squish together, and then stretch out, at the same time as the tiny hairs wiggle back and forth.

This makes a worm move.

Which end is which? Only a worm can tell. One end has a mouth, which worms use to eat tiny things such as fungus and bacteria, as well as plants and rotten animal flesh. The other end is a worm's bottom, which produces tiny worm poos. Worm poo is rich in nutrients and is wonderful food for the soil. Because of their poo, worms are gardeners' best friends! As the worms dig the soil, the soil gets mixed up and the worm poo gets mixed in, which makes the soil better to grow plants in.

Worms can live with their tails chopped off, but not their heads. An unlucky worm that's been chopped in two soon grows a new tail, but cannot grow a new head.

I really like you

Ever seen a worm as big as a tree branch? The Australian Gippsland Earthworm is over three and a half metres long!

Most worms live in the top few centimetres of soil, but they can burrow as deep as five metres. Worms are really sensitive to light, and generally move away from it, burrowing into the soil. If a worm is exposed to light for more than an hour, it becomes paralysed and can't move.

Worms love to be wet, but will drown in too much water. If it gets too dry or cold, a worm will roll into a ball, which it coats with a thick slime. It can live like this until the dry season is over. You can see all the worms coming out to celebrate after rain. Watch where you walk, these squishy, slippery, slimy things are more useful in the soil than on the underside of your shoe!

CREATIVE CATERPILLARS

Did you ever want
to become something
completely different? –
perhaps change the number of
legs you have, or grow wings?
Caterpillars do just that!

Caterpillars don't only grow wings to become
butterflies, they change in many other ways.
During metamorphosis, caterpillars form a chrysalis,
like a hard skin, around themselves, and then they
'melt' into a kind of gooey soup. The many short, fat
legs of a caterpillar become the six long, thin legs
of a butterfly. Next the hard, leaf-crunching jaws of
a caterpillar are lost and in their place forms the long,
spiral tongue of the butterfly which
is used like a straw to suck up nectar.

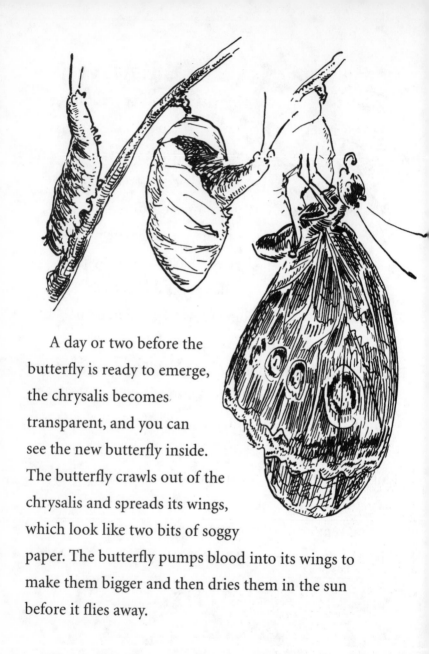

A day or two before the butterfly is ready to emerge, the chrysalis becomes transparent, and you can see the new butterfly inside. The butterfly crawls out of the chrysalis and spreads its wings, which look like two bits of soggy paper. The butterfly pumps blood into its wings to make them bigger and then dries them in the sun before it flies away.

Butterflies cannot fly if they are cold. They get most of the heat they need for flying by basking in the sun. Their wings are covered in tiny scales which are either dark so they absorb heat from the sun (just as wearing a dark shirt on a sunny day will make you hot), or light and shiny like mirrors that reflect the heat of the sun onto the butterfly's body.

The bright colours on a butterfly's wings are sometimes a warning signal, indicating that the butterfly is poisonous or will taste bad. The caterpillar of the brightly coloured Monarch Butterfly eats a poisonous plant called milkweed. Even after it has changed into a butterfly, it still has poison from the milkweed in its body and wings. Birds and other predators have learned to recognise the patterns and colours of the Monarch Butterfly and won't eat it because they know the butterfly will make them sick.

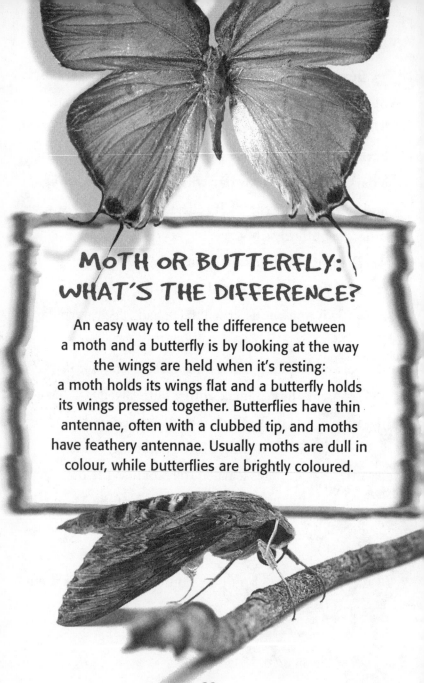

MOTH OR BUTTERFLY: WHAT'S THE DIFFERENCE?

An easy way to tell the difference between a moth and a butterfly is by looking at the way the wings are held when it's resting: a moth holds its wings flat and a butterfly holds its wings pressed together. Butterflies have thin antennae, often with a clubbed tip, and moths have feathery antennae. Usually moths are dull in colour, while butterflies are brightly coloured.

Some butterflies are not poisonous, but have wings which look the same as a poisonous butterfly's wings. This tricks predators into not eating them.

A fat, juicy caterpillar is a tasty snack to all sorts of animals. Some caterpillars protect themselves with a covering of poisonous hairs; others try and hide themselves by being the same colour as the leaves they are eating.

Hairstreak caterpillars live in herds tended by ants. The ants protect the caterpillars by chasing off predators, and the caterpillars give the ants a sweet liquid to eat. The Hook Tip Moth caterpillar scares away other caterpillars by drumming its jaws on its leaf, which makes a loud noise (for a caterpillar, anyway).

THE POO-THROWING CATERPILLAR

One particular caterpillar has a very strange way of protecting itself. The caterpillar of the Silver-spotted Skipper fires its poo up to a metre away from its body. This would be like you throwing your poo across a football field. The caterpillar builds up blood pressure in its bottom, then fires its poo far away from its leafy home.

No one was quite sure why the caterpillar did this. Some people thought it might be to keep the caterpillar free from disease, or to keep its leafy shelter from getting crowded. But we now know that this strange behaviour is to protect the caterpillar from a certain wasp. This wasp eats the caterpillars and is attracted to the smell of the caterpillar's poo. The caterpillar fires its poo as far away from where it lives as possible, so that the wasp won't know where it is.

Chapter 8

Body-snatchers

INTESTINE INVADERS

Have your parents ever made you
swallow worming tablets?
What for? You haven't
swallowed any worms
lately, have you?

Even though you
might not have swallowed
any worms, there can be some
worm-like intestine invaders inside you.

Flukes, tapeworms and roundworms are
creatures that live off other creatures – including us!

They can make us very sick. Tapeworms are flat, worm-like creatures with suckers or hooks at one end which they use to attach themselves to the wall of an intestine – the place where food is digested after it's been in the stomach.

The tapeworms live off the food passing through the intestine and grow and grow. The biggest of the tapeworms that lives in humans can reach 8 metres long – as big as the small intestine and about as long as a school bus.

Eventually they become so big that they can block up the bowel – the part of the body where food ends up. This makes the creature they're living in very sick. They can rob their host of the healthy nutrients from food until their host starves.

Parasites such as tapeworms also live in many other creatures. Tapeworms live in the water when they are young, and they spend the first part of their lives moving from host to host. They can end up in the food you eat, or living in your pets, so you have to be especially careful if you get licked on the face by an animal. They survive in animal poo, too, so it's very important to wash your hands if you go anywhere near animal poo. And next time your parents buy some worming tablets, gobble them up to make sure that a tapeworm isn't gobbling you.

Try rolling out 8 metres of toilet paper to see how long your 'small' intestine really is, and how long a tapeworm can get!

LEECHES ON THE BRAIN

Two hundred years ago, if you had a headache and went to the doctor, he probably would have put a black, slimy creature on you that sucked your blood. The black, slimy creature was a leech, and people believed that all sorts of sicknesses could be cured by leeches sucking your blood.

Leeches have jaws which are as sharp as a razor. They slit open the skin of their prey and spit on the wound. In the leech's saliva there is a chemical which stops the blood from thickening and keeps it flowing into the leech's mouth.

All leeches suck blood, but not necessarily from humans. They are parasites – like tapeworms, ticks and lice, they feed on other animals. Leeches feed on snakes, frogs, lizards, and even fish. Some leeches kill small creatures by sucking them dry, others just take a little blood then drop off. Leeches don't have to eat very often, since they can drink enough blood in one sitting to become five times their body size.

Leeches are related to earthworms, and like earthworms, have a body divided into many segments. Each segment (except for the first and the last) has its own group of nerves which, like a brain, control muscles and body functions. You could say that leeches have 32 brains!

Leeches mostly live in wet places, like lakes, puddles, or rainforests. This is because they don't have lungs like ours. Instead they absorb oxygen through a thin layer of moisture over their skin. If this layer of moisture dries out, they die. If there isn't  enough oxygen in the water, leeches rise to the surface to get oxygen from the air. Before we had sophisticated weather-predicting machines, people used to put leeches in a jar of water. If bad weather was coming, the leeches would rise to the surface. Just before storms or rains, there is a drop in pressure in the atmosphere which takes some of the oxygen out of water. The leeches then had to rise to the surface to breathe.

One doctor in the 1800s noticed that just before an electrical storm the leeches in his surgery would become agitated and restless. He built a device that was made up of 12-metre-high jars filled with water. In each jar was a leech. When the air became electrically charged, the leeches would crawl out of the water and trigger the ringing of a bell. The more bells that rang, the more likely it was that an electrical storm was on the way.

If you have just had an accident, a leech is probably the last thing you'd want stuck on you. But if it is a certain kind of injury, you may find that leeches are the best thing for you. One nine-year-old boy had his ear bitten off by a dog. The doctors sewed the ear on again, but they had to make the blood circulate through the ear or the tissue would die. Blood becomes thick and clogs up the wound when it is exposed to air (which is lucky or we would bleed to death from a small cut).

The doctors had to find a way of stopping the blood from thickening and keeping it flowing through the boy's ear to keep the tissue alive. Over a week they attached fifty leeches to the ear. The chemical in the leeches' spit kept the blood running and flowing from his head through to his ear, and the ear was successfully reattached.

So leeches could be useful to you one day. But unless you've had an accident or want to predict the weather, it's best to steer clear of those razor-sharp jaws.

EEECH!

In a battle of the slime monsters, the Horse Leech, which is found in Queensland and can grow up to 30 centimetres (as long as your school ruler), attacks and eats earthworms.

A doctor first used a leech on a patient around 2500 years ago.

The Hirudo Leech has three jaws, and each jaw has about 100 teeth. The wound from a Hirudo Leech's bite can bleed for around 10 hours.

9

Good things about bugs

Though it may seem that the world is full of tiny monsters waiting to bite, sting and eat you – it's not true! There are gazillions of bugs in the world, millions that we don't yet know anything about, and millions more we haven't even discovered. Only a very small number of bugs have a harmful effect on humans, and like all bugs, they still play an important role in keeping the environment healthy.

Without bugs, there would be few flowering plants, and no way to break down dead animal and plant matter. You can imagine how smelly the world would become! Bugs are also one of the very first links in the food chain. This means that while they eat plants and small creatures, they are in turn eaten by bigger creatures, like birds and frogs, which then become a meal for bigger creatures, like snakes and crocodiles. If you took away bugs, many animals would starve.

Bugs also help pollinate flowers, they make useful products like honey, and they eat waste products like poo, rotting meat and disease-causing bacteria. If you look closely, you'll find that many bugs are beautiful, strange and fascinating. They can do amazing things,

such as carry things hundreds of times as heavy as their body weight, jump higher and further for their body size than humans can, go for a year without food and even live for a month without their head.

So next time you see a spider next to your toilet, an ant carrying off your toast crumbs, or even a cockroach

scuttling across your kitchen counter, take a minute to appreciate them. From your bed to your toilet, bugs are **everywhere**. And even though you didn't invite them into your house, they make it a more interesting place, don't they?

HEATHER CATCHPOLE and VANESSA WOODS joined forces while working at the CSIRO because of a shared interest in bugs (insects and arthropods). Heather has been a science journalist for the ABC and the CSIRO, and is also an artist and a poet. Vanessa first became fascinated with bugs when she was about seven, when she found out how to make a mosquito explode. She now runs around the jungle in Costa Rica studying monkeys and getting to know her bugs personally (chasing cockroaches as big as her feet out of her bed, for example). She films short segments for the Disney Channel on weird, quirky and amazing animals all over the world.

CRAIG SMITH has illustrated over 300 books, including *Billy the Punk* and the *I Hate Fridays* and *Toocool* series. The humour and energy of his warm, exuberant illustrations have delighted children for over twenty-five years.

THANKS

Thanks to Kim Pullen from CSIRO Entomology, and Darren Osborne and Ross Kingsland from CSIRO's Double Helix Science Club.

And thanks to all the insects for their inspiration.

Heather Catchpole and Vanessa Woods

The publishers would like to thank BrandX Pictures for photographs used in the text, from the Bugs & Insects collection, and Dr Ken Walker, Senior Curator of Entomology at Museum Victoria in Melbourne, for checking the text.

GLOSSARY

abdomen the back part of an insect's body, where its stomach is. Our abdomens are in the middle of our body

antennae feelers attached to an insect's head that it uses to sense things in its environment

antidote a cure

anti-venom an antidote for venom

bacteria tiny life forms too small for us to see. Bacteria are found everywhere from our tummies to the toilet

camouflage markings on the body that allow an animal to blend into its environment

carnivorous meat-eating

chrysalis the cocoon used by a caterpillar as it changes into a butterfly

elytra a hard outer casing that protects beetles' wings

exoskeleton a hard outer casing that insects and other creatures like spiders have instead of a skeleton

exude produce liquid

fertilise a process that allows plants to make seeds, and animals to make eggs and babies

fungi tiny life forms distantly related to mushrooms

hermaphrodite an animal that is both male and female

host the creature that a parasite lives on

larvae the name for young insects after they hatch from eggs and before they are fully grown

metamorphosis a transformation that insects go through, as when a caterpillar turns into a butterfly

mimics copies exactly

mucus slimy stuff, such as a snail trail

omnivore an animal that eats both plants and other animals

parasite a creature that feeds on other animals

pheromones smelly chemicals used by insects and many other animals to communicate

pollinate spread pollen

predators animals that attack and eat other animals

pupa a hard outer case which an insect grows as it changes from larva to fully-grown insect

secrete make bodily fluids, as snails make slime

thorax the middle part of an insect's body

venom a poisonous substance which is injected into prey

WHERE TO FIND OUT MORE

Insect websites for curious kids

About insects for kids

- http://www.ento.csiro.au/about_insects/index.html

Australian insect common names, an identification guide

- http://www.ento.csiro.au/aicn/

The Australian National Insect Collection

- http://www.ento.csiro.au/research/natres/anic.html

Australia's spiders

- http://www.amonline.net.au/spiders/diversity/fauna/index.htm

The Australian insect farm (includes how to order your own Rhinoceros beetles)

- http://www.insectfarm.com.au/

Insects, insects, insects

- http://www.insects.org/

All about worms for kids

- http://yucky.kids.discovery.com/noflash/worm/

All about butterflies, including keeping butterflies as pets

- http://www.thebutterflysite.com/

The bug club

- http://www.ex.ac.uk/bugclub

INDEX